Contents

A kingdom without a king

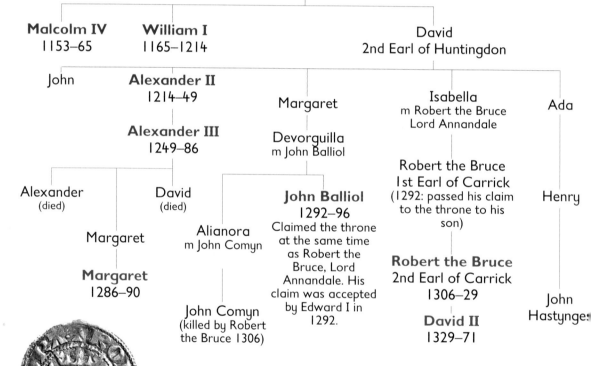

Robert the Bruce Family Tree

The rulers of Scotland from 1125–1371 are shown in red.
There were also two periods of *interregnum* (1290–92 and 1296–1306) when there was no king or queen.
The letter m means married.

David I
1125–53

Henry
1st Earl of Huntingdon

Malcolm IV
1153–65

William I
1165–1214

David
2nd Earl of Huntingdon

John

Alexander II
1214–49

Margaret

Isabella
m Robert the Bruce
Lord Annandale

Ada

Alexander III
1249–86

Devorguilla
m John Balliol

Robert the Bruce
1st Earl of Carrick
(1292: passed his claim to the throne to his son)

Alexander
(died)

David
(died)

John Balliol
1292–96
Claimed the throne at the same time as Robert the Bruce, Lord Annandale. His claim was accepted by Edward I in 1292.

Henry

Margaret

Alianora
m John Comyn

Robert the Bruce
2nd Earl of Carrick
1306–29

Margaret
1286–90

John Comyn
(killed by Robert the Bruce 1306)

David II
1329–71

John
Hastynges

Choosing a king

When Alexander III died in 1286 there was no-one to take his place as king of Scotland. The Scottish nobles asked Edward I of England to help them decide who should be the next king. The choice was between John Balliol and Robert the Bruce's grandfather, the 1st Earl of Carrick. John Balliol was chosen but he was king in name only. He did what Edward I told him.

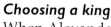

ABOVE: A silver penny showing the head of Robert the Bruce.

After three years Edward I decided to remove Balliol from the throne. He had him arrested without any reason and sent him to France. Balliol never returned. Edward I then **invaded** Scotland.

Scotland – an occupied country

Edward I and his men were cruel to the Scottish people. Englishmen were chosen to **govern** each Scottish town. They stole from the people and made their lives miserable. Many of the Scottish knights were put to death or locked up in prisons.

One brave knight, William Wallace, led the Scots against the English. He won many battles, but he was eventually captured and **executed**.

Robert the Bruce, 2nd Earl of Carrick, decided to join the Scottish knights in their fight for **independence.** He was riding to Stirling one day with John Comyn. Both Comyn and Bruce had the right to **lay claim** to the Scottish throne. During the journey they came to an agreement. One of them would try to become the new king of Scotland. The other one would get all the lands held by the families of both men.

The agreement was written down and each man marked it with his **seal**. John Comyn would be given all of Bruce's land while Bruce would become king.

LEFT:
Robert the Bruce 'was a man beautiful and of a fine appearance. His strength was so great that he could easily have overcome any mortal men of his time save one – Sir William Wallace.'

Said by Hector Boece, a Scottish historian (1465–1536).

'To be the king'

BELOW:
Scottish kings always sat upon the Stone of Destiny when they were crowned.

In 1296 Edward I took the Stone of Destiny and placed it in the English coronation chair.

Betrayal and death

John Comyn betrayed Robert the Bruce. He told Edward I about the secret agreement. Edward I told Bruce to come to the English Court. There he accused him of being **disloyal**. Bruce said this was not true, but Edward I was suspicious. He kept Bruce at the court. John Comyn wrote again to Edward I accusing Bruce. At last Edward I decided Bruce was guilty and that he must die. That night a friend sent Bruce a warning and he left secretly for Scotland. By chance he met John Comyn's servant near the Scottish border. The servant was carrying letters from Comyn to Edward I. Bruce killed the servant and took the letters. When he read them, he knew for certain that Comyn had betrayed him. He travelled to Dumfries, where he met John Comyn in Greyfriars Church.

A fight began. Bruce stabbed Comyn to death. Bruce had committed a dreadful crime. He knew that now he had to claim the Scottish crown and fight for Scotland's freedom or lose everything.

Coronation at Scone

Bruce called his men together and rode to Glasgow. Many knights who also hated the English joined him. They all went to Scone.

There Bruce was crowned on 25th March 1306 by the Bishop of Glasgow. Scottish kings were usually crowned by the Earls of Fife, but the Earl at that time was loyal to Edward I. Bruce's sister Isabella arrived after the first crowning and insisted that she must crown him again.

A king in hiding

Edward I was furious that he had been tricked by Bruce. He sent a knight, Sir Aymer de Valence, to destroy the new Scottish king. The two men met at Perth but Sir Aymer would not fight. Later that night at Methven he made a surprise attack on Bruce and his men. The Scots were outnumbered and had to run for their lives.

ABOVE:
When Bruce was in hiding he sent his wife, the Queen, and his daughter to safety at Kildrummy Castle. Later the castle was attacked by the English and burnt nearly to the ground.

LEFT:
Scone Palace – in 1306 Bruce was made king of Scotland when a gold coronet was placed on his head here.

King by right

Bruce had landed near Turnbery Castle. He found it so well defended that he decided not to attack it. Some of the English **garrison** were living outside the castle walls. Bruce and his men made a surprise attack and captured **war horses** and weapons.

Bruce realized that this was the only way he could beat the English army – through suprise attacks. Bruce's **campaign** could now begin in earnest.

ABOVE:
*Dunstaffnage, Argyll, one of the castles captured by Bruce in his two-year campaign. Its owner, Sir Alexander of Argyll, refused to pay **homage** to Bruce and fled to England.*

RIGHT:
St Andrew's Castle – this castle was held in enemy hands until after the Battle of Bannockburn had been won.

Escape and return

Bruce and his men escaped to Rathlin Island off the Irish coast. From there they travelled to the Western Isles. There, Christiania Macruarie of **Clan** Ranald gave them shelter and help. By the spring of 1307 Bruce was ready to return to mainland Scotland.

He went first of all to Arran where his men had taken clothing, weapons and food. Armed with the captured weapons, Bruce set sail for his own lands of Carrick. On returning, Bruce discovered his lands had been taken by the enemy. Even the people who lived on his land were too scared to support him openly.

On the attack

Bruce had returned to his own lands but not to his own castle. He and his followers lived in the hills and woodlands of Carrick. Bruce knew that he did not have enough men to fight an army. When a large English army tried to fight Bruce and his men at Glen Trool, Bruce **ambushed** them and defeated them. At Loudon Hill near Kilmarnock he managed to trick an army led by his old enemy, Sir Aymer de Valence.

Death of Edward I

Edward I was furious at Bruce's success. In July 1307 he marched northwards with a large army. On his way to Scotland he became very ill and died. His dying wish was that his bones would be carried ahead of the army into Scotland. Instead, Edward's son, the new king, marched the army back into England.

For the next two years Edward II remained in England and Bruce tried to take over Scotland completely. Many battles were fought. At last Bruce ruled over enough of Scotland to hold his first **parliament**. This was held at St Andrew's in March 1309.

ABOVE:
The Bruce Chapel – a chapel built at St Conan's Kirk, Loch Awe. This was the scene of a small battle fought against the men of Lorn.

ABOVE LEFT:
Loudon Hill 1307 – Bruce won the battle fought at this site by digging three deep ditches. This forced his enemies to slow down and spread out. They were then easier to attack.

Taking back the castles

The siege of Edinburgh Castle

By 1311 Bruce had captured and destroyed many of the castles held by his enemies. He had marched twice into England, destroying and **plundering** as he went. Englishmen living in the north of England were forced to pay huge amounts of money to buy peace from Bruce's army. In 1312 Bruce's nephew, Lord Thomas Randolph, set **siege** to Edinburgh Castle. The siege went on for a long time without success. Randolph finally decided that the best way to capture the castle was a surprise attack. He found a man who could lead the way up to the steep cliff on which the castle stood. On 7th June 1313, 30 men carrying ladders climbed up in the darkness. When they reached the top they placed the ladders against the castle walls and climbed over. They took the soldiers on watch and the sleeping **garrison** by surprise, capturing the castle for Bruce.

BELOW:
The steep dangerous cliffs on which Edinburgh Castle was built made it very difficult to capture.

The siege of Stirling Castle

In 1313 Edward the Bruce, Robert the Bruce's brother, laid siege to Stirling Castle. It was well defended by its keeper, Sir Philip Mowbray. When the supplies of food began to run out Mowbray suggested a **pact** to end the siege: if Edward II did not come to his aid by midsummer 1314, Mowbray would give the castle to the Scots. The pact was agreed and the siege was ended. Robert the Bruce was very angry when he heard about the pact. He knew that Edward II would use the year before June 1314 to gather men loyal to him from England, Ireland, Wales and France. The last thing that Robert the Bruce wanted was a huge army coming to attack his small Scottish **force**.

ABOVE:
If Edward II came to Stirling Castle before Midsummer's Day ended, the English could keep the castle. If he did not come, the castle would be handed over to the Scots.

Edward II kept the pact, so no battle was necessary to keep the castle.

Preparing for battle

Both armies began to prepare for battle. Soldiers were trained. Weapons were brought from abroad. Bruce made his plans. He chose the place the armies would meet with great care. This was at Torwood, near Stirling. Small trees and bushes grew on one side. On the other side the ground was marshy, full of pools, streams and ditches. A small **burn** called Bannock ran across the eastern edge. Bruce knew that the English army would have to cross the burn and the marshy ground. He and his men placed spikes in the burn, in **potholes** and in the ditches. These would cripple the horses, throwing the riders to the ground. The English army would be trapped in a narrow pass. This would greatly reduce the number of English soldiers who would reach the Scots. Bruce seemed to be in control of the battle even before it had begun.

The Battle of Bannockburn (1)

The first day

The English army of 20,000 men set out from Falkirk on Sunday 23rd June 1314. They stretched across the countryside, **breast plates** shining, banners flying – a mighty army. Robert the Bruce's army lay in wait. Bruce had divided his 5500 troops into four groups.

RIGHT:
*Sir Henry de Bohun thought King Edward II would reward him if he managed to kill Bruce. Carrying a four-metre lance he charged on his **war horse** towards Bruce.*

Bruce had been trained to deal with such an attack. He waited until the last moment. He pulled his pony's head to the left. With a back-handed movement, he struck out and up with the edge of his axe at de Bohun's lance.

He then brought the sharp edge of his axe down, cutting through de Bohun's helmet and skull.

THE BATTLE OF BANNOCKBURN
23rd JUNE 1314 [first phase]

ABOVE:
The map shows the position of the Scottish and English armies on the first day of battle.

LEFT:
Monument to Robert the Bruce at Stirling Castle.

The battle began with an attack by the English **cavalry**. The English horsemen rode towards Randolph's **division**. Randolph's men formed a **schiltrom**. The charging horses were killed by the spears. The English cavalry had to retreat. The next day the real battle began.

BELOW:
Cambuskenneth Abbey – Bruce kept his supplies here before the battle.

The Battle of Bannockburn (2)

ABOVE:
Both armies fought fiercely and bravely in the battle at Bannockburn.

The battle lasted all day until many noble knights lay slaughtered or dying on the blood-covered ground.

The second day, 24th June 1314

The Scots awoke at dawn. They took their positions on the high ground standing in four groups, or **divisions**. Three of these divisions moved to the front leaving Bruce and his men in the rear. From there Bruce could see where to send his back-up troops.

Edward II had moved his huge army across the Bannock **burn** during the night. They now stood facing the Scots across the marshy ground. Edward II did not seem to be aware that his army could be caught in a **bottleneck** and that they were walking straight into Bruce's trap. He thought that the Scots would be beaten in the first attack. His main army would then move forward.

14

"FOR · GOD · AND · ST ANDREW"

ROBERT THE BRUCE
KING OF SCOTS
PLANTED HIS STANDARD
NEAR THIS SPOT
WHEN THE
SCOTTISH PATRIOTS
UNDER HIS COMMAND
VANQUISHED THE ARMY OF
EDWARD II OF ENGLAND AT
THE BATTLE OF

BANNOCKBURN
24TH JUNE ~ 1314

CENTRE:
The statue of Robert the Bruce stands on the ground above the site of the battle. The face on the statue was made using a cast of Bruce's skull. It shows what Bruce would have looked like when he was alive.

LEFT:
This memorial marks the spot where Bruce raised his **standard** *before battle.*

Edward the Bruce's division advanced towards the English **cavalry** led by Gloucester and Hereford. Suddenly, Gloucester rushed his cavalry forward. Many of the horses were **impaled** upon the spears of the **schiltroms**. The fallen knights were killed.

Both armies fought long and hard. The English soldiers were so tightly packed together that they could not move easily. They could not kill the Scots who were within their circles of spears. They realized that they were in great danger and some of them rushed back across the Bannock burn. Bruce moved his division forward and more English troops fled. Then Edward II also left the battle field. Over the hill marched a large company of soldiers from Argyll, led by a band of fierce knights. The remaining English troops fled. The battle was won.

The struggle continues

RIGHT:
A statue of Robert the Bruce at Edinburgh Castle. It shows him with his sword and shield.

BELOW:
Archibald's Tower, Threave Castle, was built in 1360 by Archibald the Grim, son of James Douglas. It stands on an island in the River Dee.

After Bannockburn

Edward II and 500 horsemen rode from the battlefield to Stirling Castle. The keeper, Sir Philip Mowbray, refused to let them in. He knew that the castle would soon be handed over to the Scots. He told Edward II to make his escape to Berwick, which he did.

Many of the captured English knights were used as **ransom** for Scottish prisoners. Bruce's wife, Elizabeth, his daughter Marjorie and the Bishop of Glasgow were returned in exchange for the Earl of Hereford.

Battle and raids

Although the Scots had won the battle at Bannockburn and Bruce was in control of his kingdom, the fighting carried on. Edward II controlled Wales and Ireland. He did not want to admit that Scotland was **independent.** The Scots had to remain on their guard. They attacked wherever and whenever they could to keep their country safe.

English troops **occupied** Ireland. Robert the Bruce's brother, Edward the Bruce, went there with his troops. He managed to capture a large area. He had himself crowned king of Ireland. Robert the Bruce took 600 of his best troops to Ireland to help his brother but because of **famine** there he returned to Scotland. The Scots who remained in Ireland were defeated by a large English army. Edward the Bruce was killed.

On the border

At this time battles and raids took place in the border country. James Douglas captured the castles of Wark, Harbottle, Mitford and Berwick. When Edward II tried to recapture Berwick Castle he failed and returned to England.

ABOVE:
Caerlaverock Castle was captured by Edward I in 1300 and given to Sir Eustace Maxwell. Maxwell decided to support the Scots and made the castle a ruin.

A call for freedom

RIGHT:
Pope John XXII did not reply to the Declaration of Arbroath until 1324. He then recognized Bruce as king of Scotland.

FAR RIGHT:
Bruce hid in this cave in Arran. It is said that here he watched a spider trying again and again to reach a certain part of its web. It did not give up until it had done so. Bruce decided that he too would 'try, try, try' again to win Scotland's freedom.

RIGHT:
Arbroath Abbey, where, in April 1320, Scottish nobles met and agreed to protest because the Pope would not recognize Bruce as king.

Treason

The Pope did not reply to the declaration immediately. In the meantime, some of the nobles who signed the document proved to be dishonest. They began to plot against Bruce. One of them, William of Soulis, wanted to be king. When Bruce found out about the plot he called a **parliament** at Scone. There several of the Scottish nobles, including Soulis, were found guilty of **treason**. They were imprisoned or killed.

The Declaration of Arbroath

In 1319 a two-year **truce** was agreed between Scotland and England. Scotland could not become **independent** until the Pope in Rome recognized Bruce as the Scottish king. He had refused to do so because Bruce killed John Comyn in Greyfriars Church. In 1320 the Scottish nobles and bishops met together at Arbroath Abbey. All the nobles signed a **declaration** written to the Pope. In it the Scots declared that most Scottish people wanted Bruce to continue as their king. They also declared that they considered Edward II an enemy and would never allow him to rule over them.

Under attack

When the truce between the two countries ended in 1322, Edward II **invaded** Scotland again. He attacked and destroyed Holyrood Abbey. When he searched for food he discovered that Bruce had taken all the meat and corn away from the area around Edinburgh. All Edward II could do was to retreat. He went to Melrose Abbey.

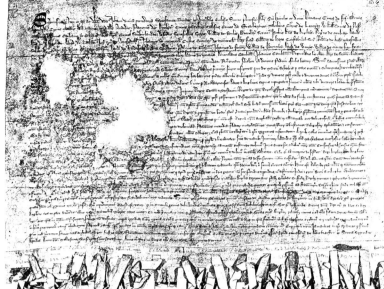

There he and his troops were scattered by James Douglas. Bruce decided to take the battle into England. He marched with his army southwards until he met Edward II's army. He defeated them and returned to Scotland with weapons, **siege towers** and **hostages**.

ABOVE:
*In the Declaration of Arbroath the Scots wrote that 'the kingdom of Scots had been governed by an uninterrupted succession of 113 kings all of our own nature and royal stock... we will never give consent to subject ourselves to the **dominion** of the English.'*

Peace

ABOVE:
This is the beginning of a charter given to the people of Carlisle by Edward II. He gave it to them after they stopped Robert the Bruce from capturing the town in 1315 by bravely fighting against him for ten days.

In 1327 Edward II argued with his English nobles and his son Edward III was made king in his place. In June 1327 Bruce sent another army into England. This army attacked and burned as it marched. The following year another Scottish army attacked yet again. The English began to realize that they could not win.

A **peace treaty** was drawn up. In the Treaty of Northampton the English were forced to admit that Bruce and his **descendants** were kings of Scotland. They agreed to a marriage between Bruce's son David and Princess Joanna Plantagenet, the sister of Edward III. Both sides were to protect each other in the time of war. Edward III was to do all he could to get the Pope to forgive Bruce for killing John Comyn.

The peace which Bruce had fought for was at last won. Also, with the birth of his son David, in 1324, he had an **heir** to the throne in Scotland. However, Bruce himself was very ill and had just over one year to live.

Bruce's Death – 1329

It is often thought that Bruce died of leprosy. He had a skin
disease called red leprosy, that is now known as **dermatitis**.
This would not have killed him. He may have died from **dropsy**.
Before he died in 1329 he asked that his heart should be taken to
Jerusalem in the Holy Land. He wanted all his sins to be
forgiven, especially the killing of Comyn. James Douglas set out,
carrying Bruce's heart in a **silver casket**. During a battle against
the Saracens, Douglas was killed. Bruce's heart was returned to
Scotland. It was buried in Melrose Abbey. Bruce's son, David II,
became the next king.

In Scotland today Bruce's courage and daring are not forgotten.
Nor will they be – he was a strong and brave king.

Glossary

ambush – attack from a hiding place

bottleneck – a narrow place that stops people from moving easily from one area to another

breast plate – a piece of armour worn by knights to protect their chests

burn – a small stream

campaign – a series of attacks planned to win freedom or land

cavalry – troops riding on horseback

clan – a word used in the Scottish Highlands to describe a group of families who are loyal to one chief

declaration – an announcement

dermatitis – a disease of the skin that makes it red and flaky

descendants – sons, daughters, grandchildren or their children

disloyal – no longer faithful to a person or cause

division – a group or unit of soldiers in an army, that may be divided into smaller groups for training

dominion – cruel and harsh rule

dropsy – disease in which water collects in parts of the body

executed – put to death, killed

famine – a shortage of food

force – a group of soldiers

garrison – a group of soldiers living in a fort or castle to defend it

govern – to rule over or keep under control

heir – person who takes on a person's possessions or position when that person dies

homage – show respect or honour

hostage – someone held by another person to force someone else to bargain

impaled – pierced by a sharp point

independence – not belonging to other people or another country

invade – to enter a country with an army

lay claim to the throne – to claim the right to rule over a country or people

occupied – a country that is ruled and lived in by soldiers from another country

pact – a bargain or agreement

parliament – a meeting of nobles, bishops and free men who make laws

peace treaty – an agreement to make peace

plunder – to take things that belong to other people by force, during a war

pothole – a deep hole in a stream

ransom – the release of a person or property in return for another person or for money

schiltrom – a tightly packed circular wall of spears

seal – a stamp or ring that is pressed into soft wax to leave the owner's sign **siege** – surround a castle with armed men and not let anyone enter or leave

siege tower – wooden tower holding ladders, used to climb castle walls

silver casket – a small box made from silver

standard – flag or banner

treason – an attempt to remove a king from a throne

truce – an agreement to stop a war for a short time

war horses – large horses used to carry knights into battle

Timeline 1286–1329

1286 1287 1288 1289 1290 1291 1292 1293 1294

John Balliol claims the Scottish throne. His claim is accepted.

Alexander III dies after a riding accident at Burntisland in Fife.

Margaret, granddaughter of Alexander III, dies in Orkney of sea-sickness. No obvious heir to the Scottish throne.

1303 1302 1301 1300 1299 1298 1297 1296 1295

The Battle of Stirling Bridge – a victory for the Scots led by Sir William Wallace against the English.

John Balliol is forced to give up the throne. Edward I attacks Scotland.

1304 1305 1306 1307 1308 1309 1310 1311 1312

Sir William Wallace is executed in London.

Robert the Bruce murders John Comyn in Greyfriars Church, Dumfries. Bruce claims the Scottish throne.

Robert the Bruce holds his first Parliament in St Andrews.

The siege of Edinburgh Castle – 30 men led by Randolph take the castle.

Robert the Bruce defeats the English at the Battle of Loudon Hill. Edward I dies on his way to Scotland.

1321 1320 1319 1318 1317 1316 1315 1314 1313

The Declaration of Arbroath – Scotland claims its independence.

The Battle of Bannockburn – Edward II is defeated by the Scots.

1322 1323 1324 1325 1326 1327 1328 1329 1330

The Treaty of Northampton for peace is signed between Scotland and England.

Robert the Bruce dies. His son David II succeeds to the throne.

Index